THE GOOD BUG BOOK...

(And Other Cool Creatures)

Paul Calabrese

To order additional copies of this book, contact:
Xlibris
844-714-8691
www.Xlibris.com
Orders@Xlibris.com

ISBN: Softcover   978-1-4797-4131-1
        Hardcover   978-1-4797-4132-8
        EBook   978-1-4797-4133-5

Library of Congress Control Number: 2012920335

Print information available on the last page

Rev. date: 09/03/2021

In *The Bad Bug Book,* the author Paul Calabrese introduces
us to annoying pests that bug us terribly but have no fear . . .
The Good Bug Book (and Other Cool Creatures) is here.
The Good Bug Book looks at good bugs that are beneficial
to our environment, and it also looks at other cool
creatures that benefit our lives in some way every day.

Author Biography

Author of The Bad Bug Book, Paul Calabrese, was born
in Yonkers, New York, in 1968 and raised in Brooklyn,
New York. He is the current owner of Abolish Pest Control
Services Inc., servicing the New York City area.

Ashley the
Ambush Bug

The ambush bug is really slick,
And might be disguised as a stick.
They hide so well, a real cool trick,
To ambush their prey, super quick.

A butterfly is quite a sight,
With different colors of patterns bright.
In the park where we play,
They help make it a beautiful day.

Bella the
Butterfly

Nestled in branches as safe as can be,
Caterpillars build cocoons as you may see.
And there they sleep as time goes by,
And soon become a butterfly.

Carmine the Caterpillar

Crickets like to play at night,
And hide so well out of sight.
They're tough to catch if you wish,
But their familiar chirping cannot be missed.

Cody the Cricket

Dragonflies are helpful guys,
They eat mosquitoes, ants, and flies.
By the wetlands they're often found,
Where they keep their newborns
safe and sound.

Dameon the
Dragonfly

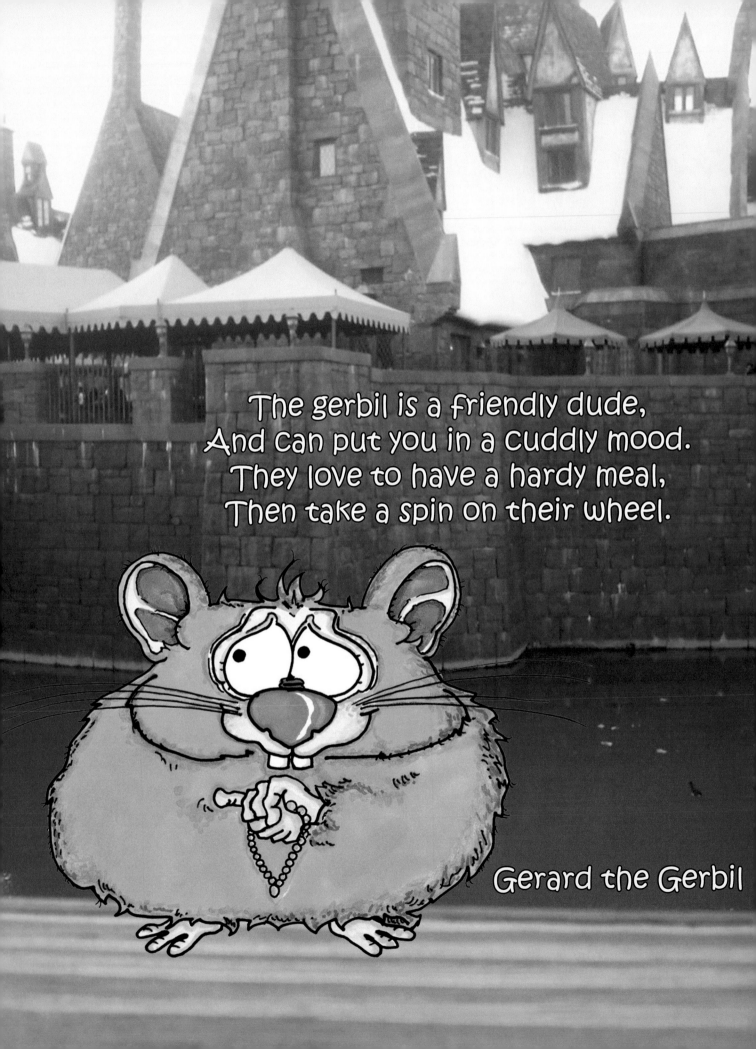

The gerbil is a friendly dude,
And can put you in a cuddly mood.
They love to have a hardy meal,
Then take a spin on their wheel.

Gerard the Gerbil

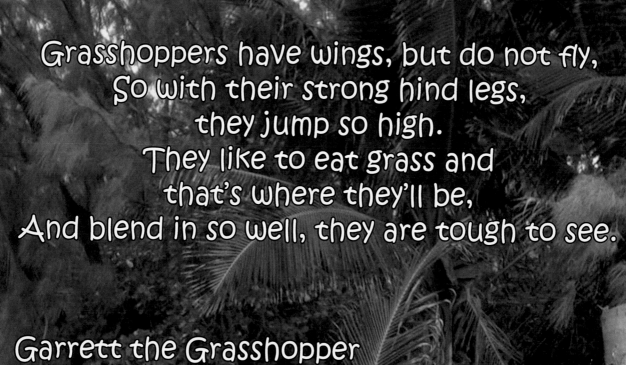

Grasshoppers have wings, but do not fly,
So with their strong hind legs,
they jump so high.
They like to eat grass and
that's where they'll be,
And blend in so well, they are tough to see.

Garrett the Grasshopper

Halley the
Honey Bee

Honeybees help the flowers,
And pollinate some crops of ours.
They also produce and provide honey,
Which most people say tastes really yummy.

A popular bug lady bugs are,
And can be found from near to far.
They flaunt their beauty, which brings us joy,
But a lady bug might be a boy.

Linda the Lady Bug

Lizards have been here for very long,
Two hundred million years and going strong.
Some change colors to blend right in,
Some run on water instead of swim.

Louie the Lizard

Lightning bugs are fun to catch,
Just make sure you put them back.
Where they belong is in the air,
Spreading there light everywhere.

Laddie the Lightning Bug

Every single thing on earth,
Must be made of molecules first.
From bats to bugs, from cars to corn,
It's molecules that give us form.

Minnie the Molecule

Pirate bugs are helpful mates,
They keep our gardens looking great.
They eat the bad bugs that crawl around,
To keep our gardens safe and sound.

Paulie the Pirate Bug

The praying mantis is fierce indeed,
On other bugs in which it feeds.
So respect this bug and look in awe,
because hurting one is against the law.

Pedro the
Praying Mantis

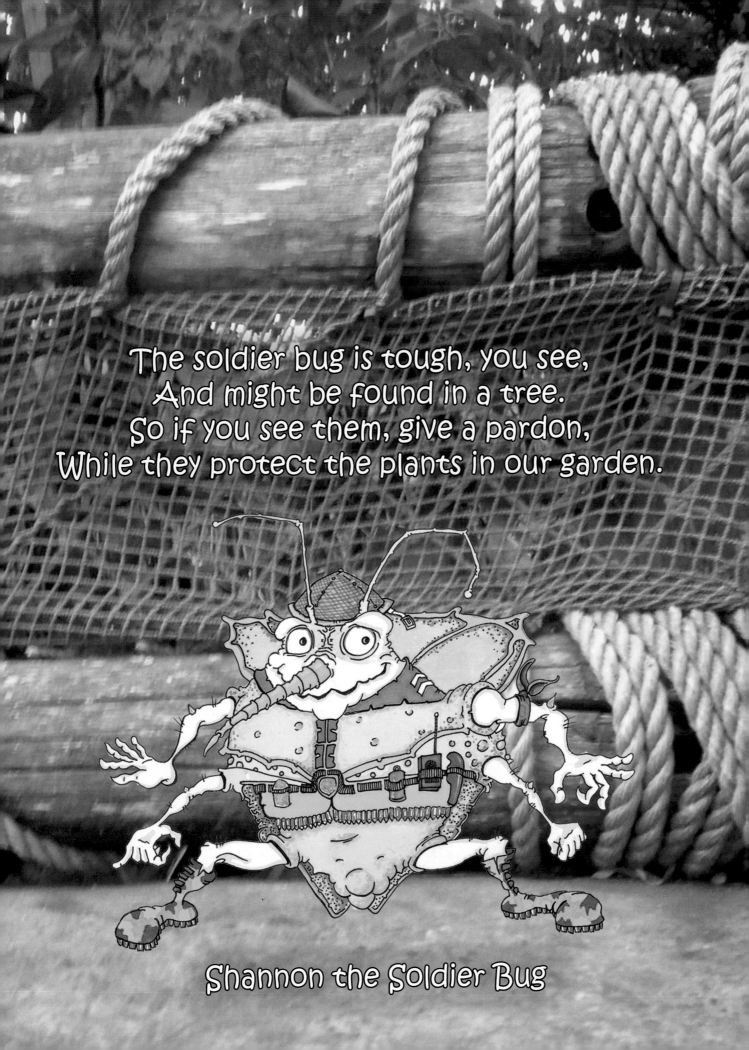

The soldier bug is tough, you see,
And might be found in a tree.
So if you see them, give a pardon,
While they protect the plants in our garden.

Shannon the Soldier Bug

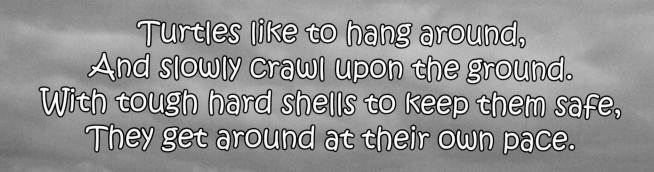

Turtles like to hang around,
And slowly crawl upon the ground.
With tough hard shells to keep them safe,
They get around at their own pace.

Tony the Turtle